THE LITTLE BOOK OF PYRAMID INTUITION

Amethyst Gray
Steve Nicholls

To Lauren
Enjoy! x
Amethyst x

The characters and events portrayed in this book are fictitious. Any similarity to real persons, living or dead, is coincidental and not intended by the author.

ISBN-13: 978-1-9162128-7-9

Cover design by: A. Hargreaves

To those who seek truth in all its forms.

CONTENTS

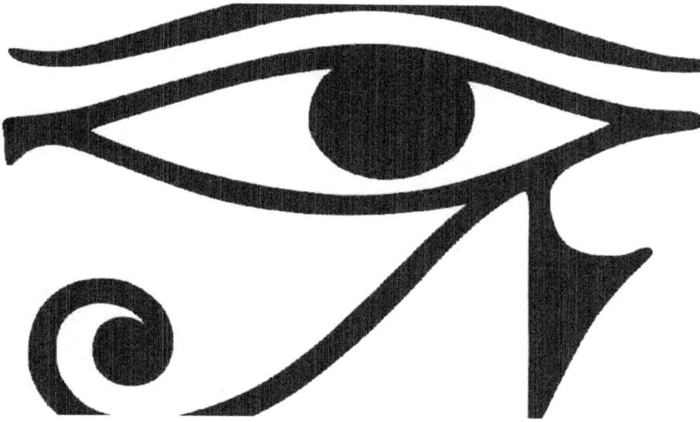

WHAT IS INTUITION?

By Amethyst Gray

Intuition is defined as '*The faculty of knowing or understanding something without reasoning or proof.*'

But how do we 'know' something of this nature?

For me, it is a calm sense of knowing that I feel in my heart.

Sometimes this is easier said than done as we make our way through the 'real world' of life in a 3D plane.

The stresses and strains of everyday life can cloud our judgement, separate us from our higher selves or put us into a fight-or-flight fear-response.

I remember a quote from one of my favourite pieces of science fiction – Frank Herbert's Dune - when I think of a fear mindset:

"I must not fear. Fear is the mind-killer. Fear is the little-death that brings total obliteration. I will face my fear. I will permit it to pass over me and through me. And when it has gone past I will turn the inner eye to see its path. Where the fear has gone there will be nothing. Only I will remain."

Intuition flows when you are in a place of calm. This doesn't need to be physically calm, more mentally. If we can calm ourselves, trust in a higher good despite the terrible events that might be going on in the wider world, then we can move past our fears and access our true intuition.

For calming exercises, I would recommend 'The Little Book of Pyramid Meditation'. The exercises in there will help still your mind, calm your heart, reduce your stress levels and bring you towards a place where you can access your intuition.

When writing, painting or doing other forms of creativity, including computer coding or knowledge work, you can access a higher plane of consciousness. This plane is sometimes called 'The Zone'. Athletes, professional sportspeople and even racing drivers can all enter this state of mind. Actions and reactions become automatic, graceful, perhaps even fluid. Driving alone over long distances can also have this effect.

Accessing 'The Zone' is undoubtedly one way of accessing your intuition.

But it is not the only way. If you can tune into that inner knowing, act upon its advice and learn to trust it, your intuition will be available to you most of the time.

I say 'most of the time' as we can all fall back into a primal fear mindset at times. When we feel helpless, our inner demons can swamp out our intuition and fool us.

Intuition only comes from a place of purity. Our inner demons of greed, avarice, envy, pride, sloth, gluttony and pride – also known as the seven deadly sins – can wash away our good intentions.

Decisions made in conjunction with our inner demons are those that lead to consequences.

Karma will be triggered as a result. And action leads to some reaction. Karma means 'action'.

Bad decisions lead to dire consequences for us in this lifetime or the next. In our current epoch, we can see that the consequences are coming back sooner and more extreme than at any time in our history.

THE INTUITIVE 'HUNCH'

By Steve Nicholls

Understanding and enabling one's intuition in any situation is something that can be a different experience from one person to another.

As we have discussed in our previous books, we feel that meditation is a good way of working with one's intuition, and to that end, pyramid meditation as described in our previous work may be accessed and utilised. It is not the only way, however – and I firmly feel that whatever works best for a person is largely dependent on their own senses and ways of doing things. An intuitive 'hunch' that proves to be correct often appears to be a rare and unpredictable event. However, I have discovered that this is not necessarily the case and as with many things, consistent and diligent practice can prove very interesting and fruitful.

Have you ever gone against a 'gut feeling' that eventually proves to have been an incorrect action to have taken?

With two events in my own life, I went against immediate and persistent hunches that things would not go well for me if I pursued these courses. Both unfortunately resulted in car accidents – although very luckily on both occasions no-one was injured – but my cars were damaged. With the first accident, many years ago, I was on holiday to Scotland with my wife and my eldest daughter who was very young. We had had a wonderful time, but on the way back, we made an error and ended up driving through the centre of Glasgow. That morning, before setting off I had the strongest instinct that something awful was going to happen that day. I just couldn't shake it off, but felt that I should not be driving that morning. However, I went against that and although my wife could drive, I felt I should take the longest stretch and we set off. Quite how we got into the centre of Glasgow, I am not sure. This was well before the days of sat-navs and on what appeared to be a complicated road system, I must have missed a by-pass. As we got into the centre, there was a huge box junction with traffic lights and I waited until both the lights were green and I could see my way through. However the junction wasn't straightforward and a car had turned into it. My line of sight was partially blocked by a double-decker bus obscuring the road behind it and facing me. The driver waved me on for me to take my route and as I reluctantly did so; that niggling intuition suddenly becoming overpoweringly strong. Before I could react a car came from behind and adjacent to the bus and hit the passenger side and then rear of my car with some force. Miraculously my wife and daughter were fine, although badly shaken, as was I. I got out and checked the other driver who was a heavily pregnant woman. As I was ensuring that the woman seemed to be uninjured, the police arrived. No-one stopped though and there were many potential witnesses. The bus driver and his vehicle had vanished which I suppose was not surprising as no doubt he didn't want to be questioned about the incident; nor of his hand-signalling for me to enter that junction! My car was very badly damaged and the passenger side headlight somehow had also been hit. However, when I told the police officer that I needed to get home, in England and the accident had occurred quite early in the morning with many hours of daylight left, he actually let me proceed – with the instructions that if I was stopped, I was to give his number etc. and that he had let me continue my journey. Very kind of him really – but the whole thing was a potentially life-threatening event. The pregnant woman was taken to hospital to be checked over, and it seems that she and her baby were thankfully uninjured. For some time afterwards I felt guilty for not going with my strong intuition that my wife should have been driving for that part of the journey. If I had gone with that gut feeling though and had she driven, would the same thing have occurred? My senses seemed to indicate that we would have got home without incident, but of course we would never have known.

The second incident was much closer to home and both my wife and I this time (even stating it to each other that we felt 'something') didn't want to take a detour because of the road being closed off due to another accident. Unfortunately, we had no choice and sure enough the same kind of thing happened, but that time, relatively minor damage occurred to our vehicle.

I have invariably found though that an instinctive hunch or intuition when not followed, leads to tricky circumstances. I have had that with a job interview, with decisions with money; repairs to our house – and all kinds of other things. If I follow my intuition, all is fine but if I don't...well!

This raises the point then of how to really understand and use the intuitive sense wisely. As stated above it really is difficult, but deciding to act on hunches quickly can prevent many undesirable situations from occurring. When analysing this it feels as if there are two paths one can take, and the second, often logical one is not necessarily correct. Hunches are feelings, and are not controlled by the mind. That initial strong sense can appear to vanish very quickly, within a second or less as another sense – that of logic and rational thought kicks in. This is the brain's way of filtering as through our lives we are conditioned to think in all situations.

Amethyst has given a detailed account of how intuition may be accessed and acted upon, primarily using the focus of a constructed pyramid, or an imagined one. She also mentioned Karma as giving faster responses than, as she states, any other time in history. While I certainly do not disagree with that, as with many things considering metaphysics, the difficulty tends to be with proving it. My own intuitive senses are that we are indeed at a point where reactions happen quickly, but if we were to be able to travel back in time and ask people who experienced a reaction to a sense and whether a Karmic response to an undesirable decision came quickly or not, I suspect that for many it may be so. We must remember also that the population of Earth is much greater, and therefore many more people may be experiencing reactions quickly. Whatever the truth, we both feel that Karma, as Amethyst gave in her definition of it, certainly occurs.

Karma, though, I sense is not a tricky thing to have to navigate. Many people think that Karmic 'laws' apply to us through whatever action we have undertaken in previous lives. Again, I have a different perspective on this, and this is purely based on an intuitive feel of course. My sense is that we may experience all manner of things simultaneously at a far deeper level than that which we are consciously aware of. I feel that we continuously apply a learning pattern to whatever we may experience. If we take a decision that is, for example, not a morally effective one; most of us will be aware of that, often as a nagging prick at our consciousness. We may then use our intuition hopefully not to repeat that, as the sense that it is 'wrong' will be strong within our psyche. Even if the sense of something as not being right is buried within our unconscious aspect, I feel that it is worked on and not applied elsewhere, or even 'else when'. By this, I mean that if our consciousness is part of a whole, and consciousness is the instigator of energy, well, energy has been shown to be affecting itself, theoretically across the universe. What is more, quantum physics has demonstrated that an electron can become 'entangled', affecting its twin instantaneously, even across the universe. For me, this indicates that consciousness must therefore be everywhere, and if we define ourselves as part of that consciousness, it means that time as we understand it, is really a construct. Therefore, if consciousness resides everywhere, it means that our conscious mind is everywhere, and even the electrons in our bodies 'entangle' with other electrons. That might be at the far edge of the known universe!

If we accept this as a possibility, then it becomes easier to also understand how intuition works, and even how we can learn to recognise it, encourage its form within our consciousness, and exploit that aspect to work properly for us.

This, I imagine, is a lifetime's study; or many lifetimes if we accept the theory I gave above. So, what can we do about this? What forms can intuition take to be properly acted upon in a positive and beneficial way?

SYNCHRONICITY AND INTUITION

By Steve Nicholls

One thing I and some friends have noticed is that synchronicities become frequent when one has a receptive and open mind. I have found that synchronicity and intuition are closely related. Synchronicity may be defined as coincidence with purpose, or meaning. Often an initial unrelated event may occur which gives rise to a synchronicity. To give one example of this, I am in communication by e-mail or telephone very occasionally with a writer whose books are fascinating studies of the mind. Sometimes though very long periods can go without us contacting each other, but I recall many years ago having a sense that I should contact my author friend. I decided straight away to send an e-mail to him, asking him how he was and how his writing was going. Within half an hour, I received a reply back from him. He was astounded as he had just published a book about coincidences and synchronicity and he was about to contact me to send me a copy as he had included an incident of lucid dreaming I had described to him some time before. Imagine our astonishment at the synchronicity of this – a book about synchronicity itself! What had actually occurred here? My best understanding is that Tony had sent a thought to me by some kind of telepathic process, and the energy of that, of it being foremost in his mind to send me a copy of his book had nudged me to act on a hunch – an intuition – that I had to contact him after a gap of over two years.

This raises another question. Are there different elements of intuitive hunches, working in slightly different ways? So, for example, is one aspect an intuitive meeting of minds at a precise time? I am inclined to think that this is true. To give another personal example. I am by profession, a musician. Some years ago I had a band where there were two main songwriters; myself and a singer/songwriter. What we discovered after a few weeks of writing together was that more often than not we would work out a chord sequence immediately together, without one taking the lead from the other, even selecting the same key at the same time. Now, initially, I was convinced that as we liked the same styles of music, it was likely that we had locked into a way of writing where we instinctively sensed a harmonic structure and common chords and progressions to use. One day though we picked up our guitars and without a word played through a complex sequence of complicated jazz chords and progressions. This was bizarre as neither of us were jazz musicians, or particularly interested in that genre. I may have had a slight leaning to it out of the two of us as I am classically trained, but again, I had never written in that style before.

This served to make me think how to consciously tap into this aspect, as I considered it must be possible by virtue of it actually occurring, albeit at a different level than that of conscious awareness. As I thought about this, it became clear that when I had worked on aspects of willing something to happen many years before, when I was a child, after I applied concentration to a subject over a number of days whenever I could focus my attention to this, the solution to a problem would happen often after I let go of the situation from my mind. This applied to schoolwork; to aspects of what I might be thinking of with my family – for example often during the summer holidays we would have coach journeys to the coast and my mother would never tell us when they would be because she would book and surprise my sister and me. However, I would suddenly be thinking 'seaside' or 'trip' a couple of days before. The imagery of that would be completely in my mind, and then something would distract me from that intense thought and I would relax. Very soon (within hours) of that happening, my mother would suddenly exclaim that we were going to the seaside or some other trip the next day or two. This happened for several years from the age of about nine to fourteen and I would never know when or if we were going anywhere at that point. Now, it may be argued that expectation of a trip had been placed one year because that is what happened the first year. That may be the case indeed, but the regularity of this occurring – and sometimes there were several day trips during the summer holidays – combined with other aspects of intuitive reasoning, or awareness, has made me consider that in the balance of probabilities, it may be that I was telepathically keying into my mother's awareness and planning of such an event.

I am giving examples of my own understandings of intuition and how it may work in the hope that the methods I have employed may assist you too.

Although, when I was a young child I hadn't keyed into pyramids or even thought about them. What initially triggered my curiosity, quite apart from (or perhaps a synchronicity there too with my formative meeting with Anubis, as described in 'The Little Book of Pyramids), was an episode of the British science fiction series 'Doctor Who' that really caught my imagination at the time. It was aired from the 25th October 1975 when I would have been 11 years old. Pyramids became suddenly a focus point of my awareness, notwithstanding the somewhat creepy plot. It was the link in with Egypt that held my fascination although at that stage I really didn't understand why. Now, I think I do; as I have written about in our first book in this series.

Pyramids are, as we have described a really good source of meditation. The shape and the energy that many people feel able to discern, myself included, serve to allow a meditative point of concentration.

Using this form, either held in your mind's eye, or by sitting inside a constructed pyramid, by allowing the focus to just centre, I feel that it aides in bringing a clarity and awareness to a situation that may then nudge the intuition to give an insightful response. Clarity is the key here – concentration on the shape, by holding the awareness at the point (with eyes closed) behind the forehead allows the 'third eye' to open and from that, clarity can ensue and intuition becomes developed. This, however, often takes many sessions before effects can be noticed. Having a goal in mind is the useful thing here. However, thinking of things that may be impacting an area of your life in a tricky way does not seem to bring the desired result. As an example, focusing one's attention on money, just for its own sake, seems to be a desire that is not based on a positive outcome. Dickens may well have been onto something when he wrote about the miserly Scrooge and his obsession to the point of ignoring the positive values of his own psyche. Again, this is the thing: awareness of focus to one's good is about the good of the psyche; or the soul, if you like. Have you noticed that we are happiest when we are not completely self-absorbed? We only have to look at children playing to see this. They may appear to be completely self-absorbed; but if they are happy, that self-absorption is bringing in a positive aspect to them, and very often to other children and adults around them. The joy of being immersed in what we positively enjoy doing brings its reward. Perhaps become, as an intuitive process made me write once, 'the child of your mind'.

This then is the true aspect of intuition. It can serve to protect us from a dangerous situation, if we have the ability to both recognise and then act on that recognition, but it can also propel us to become aware of really meaningful synchronicities that allow us to look at ourselves in a clearly positive and perhaps enlightened way.

I will leave you to reflect on this message from Anubis that came to my mind intuitively and without deep conscious thought and I wish you all joy as you explore your intuition. The tools we have given here may help you in your journey.

'When you can watch a snowflake un-melt in your hand

Or sense the lonely call of the gull –

When you become the child of your mind,

Then you will truly know yourself.'

(Anubis/ S.P. Nicholls)

THE HOME OF YOUR INTUITION

By Amethyst Gray

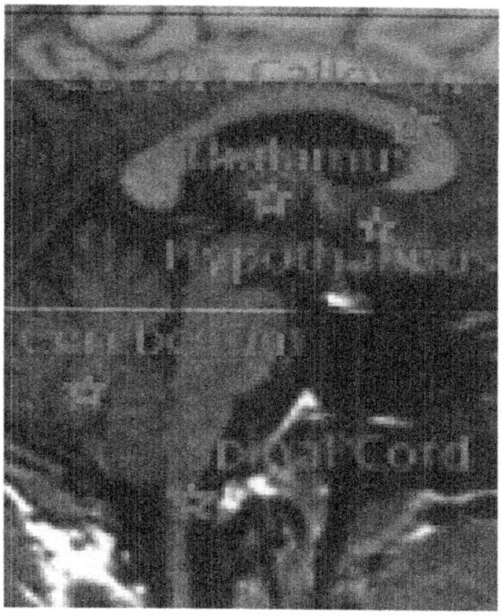

It is not by accident that the temple complexes in Ancient Egypt featured hieroglyphs of the Eye of Horus, or sometimes the very similar Eye of Ra.

The Pineal Gland is the seat of our intuition and inner knowing. When human brains have been sliced through, the similarity of the Eye of Horus to the constituent parts of the inner brain is unmistakable. The top' eyebrow' is the Corpus Callosum, the eye itself is the Thalamus, the corner of the eye is the pineal gland, the vertical line below the eye is the Hypothalamus, and the curled 'tail' leading back from the eye is the Cerebellum behind the spinal cord.

The 'third eye' is thus a physical eye of sorts. As the Eye of Ra is the Sun's eye, it can be said that our third eye is our inner Sun, the seat of our intuition.

Sadly, our pineal gland is often found to be calcified or vitrified through lack of use and impurities in our environment, such as calcium or fluoride in the water.

However, meditation and tuning into our intuition can bring it back into use and free it from its dormant state.

The Eye of Horus was the emblem of protection, royal power, and good health.

THE HISTORY OF INTUITION

By Amethyst Gray

The Mystery Schools of Ancient Egypt taught their adepts to tune into their bodies, master their thoughts, and calm their emotions. In so doing, they were fully able to access their intuition.

The concept of the Jedi from the science fiction series 'Star Wars' was taken from the Djedd Pillars found in Ancient Egypt.

In the story of Osiris and Isis, Osiris was killed by

his brother Set through being tricked into going inside a coffin made to fit Osiris exactly. Set then had the coffin with the deceased Osiris flung into the Nile. The Nile carried the coffin to the ocean and on to the city of Byblos in Syria. Unfortunately, it ran aground, and a sacred tree took root and rapidly grew around the coffin, enclosing the coffin within its trunk. The King of the land, intrigued by the tree's rapid growth, ordered the tree to be cut down and installed as a pillar in his palace, unaware that the tree contained Osiris's body.

Meanwhile, Isis searched for Osiris aided by Anubis and came to know of Osiris's location in Byblos. Isis manoeuvred herself into the favour of the King and Queen and was granted a wish. She asked to be given the pillar in the palace hall, and upon being granted it, extracted the coffin from the pillar. She then consecrated the pillar, anointing it with myrrh and wrapping it in linen. This pillar came to be known as the pillar of Djedd.

In Egyptian mythology, by raising the Djedd Pillar, Osiris is returned from the dead. (The raising of the dead).

In metaphysics, Osiris is the Lord of the Underworld and is symbolic to your subconscious mind.

By raising the Djedd Pillar - the energy within your spine - you can override your conscious mind to access the most powerful force within you, the subconscious mind of your intuition. In so doing, you can quell your human nature and restore order to your universe.

'Mr Spock' from 'Star Trek' is adept at doing the same thing through his Vulcan upbringing, though the writers substitute logic with intuition since intuition can appear more chaotic than the order of logic.

The Djedd pillar represents stability. The Ancient Egyptians maintained that Djedd pillars were in the four corners of the Earth and kept it in place.

The Djedd pillar can also be pictured with arms or wings supporting a disc, usually thought to represent the Sun disc of Ra.

HOW TO TUNE INTO YOUR INTUITION

By Amethyst Gray

You can tune into your intuition in its purest form. It is best to calm your body and tune into a place of purity within yourself or outside of yourself.

In our book 'The Little Book of Pyramids', we explained what pyramids are and how you can make use of them or even make one of your own.

By tuning into a pyramid, you are connecting with a structure that is sitting upon the surface of Gaia, our Earth mother and is itself accessing the pure energy of our planet.

To tune into the power of the pyramid to access your intuition, look at or visualise in your mind the top of the pyramid – the pyramidion (or the keyring piece from 'The Little Book of Pyramids' structure).

Once you are tuned into that, visualise a Djedd / spinal pillar descending from the apex to the floor beneath the apex of the pyramid.

Once that is firmly planted in your mind, you can trace (imagine) energy surging up from the ground (Gaia) towards the apex (Ra). Ideally, the energy should spiral up clockwise (anti-clockwise is also OK).

Now trace/imagine energy surging down from the apex (Ra/the sky) towards the ground/Gaia. Again, ideally, this energy should spiral down anti-clockwise (clockwise is OK as long as the other component is the opposite).

This flow completes the healing Caduceus circuit and allows you to raise your consciousness, increase your vibration and access your intuition.

This exercise can be a very heady, spacey experience, so please keep grounding crystals such as black obsidian, tourmaline or shungite to hand along with a glass of water to allow you to ground afterwards.

This practice is a form of 'Illumination'. Once you have learned this technique to access your intuition, you will be able to repeat it again and again.

Each time it will become easier and easier until you can access your intuition without explicitly invoking it.

As stated in an earlier chapter, use this method responsibly and ensure that you come from a place of purity before tuning into your intuition.

Like dowsing, tarot cards or crystal pendants, ' divining' must be used for your highest good and for that of those for whom you are asking the questions of your intuition. Anything less can skew your conclusions—*caveat emptor.*

HOW TO ENHANCE YOUR INTUITION

By Amethyst Gray

Your mind is like a pyramid or tower in itself. Therefore, to enhance your intuition, it is necessary to clear all stray thoughts and concerns.

Sit under your pyramid if you have one, or otherwise find a quiet spot where you won't be disturbed. Play some calming music if that helps you or otherwise sit in total silence.

Steady your breathing into a comfortable pattern where you are taking long, relaxing, deep breaths. Keep your breath steady for 2-3 minutes before closing your eyes to go inwards to your mind.

Imagine that your mind is a pyramid or tower where each thought has to cross through a central cube of empty space. Bring your concentration to bear on that empty cube. As thoughts come into mind attempting to cross that cube, you should acknowledge them but keep them out of the cube. This process may take a short while. Keep the cube clear for a minute or so before introducing the question or problem that requires your intuition to consider. Then, as the question or problem is introduced, let it drift around in the cube within your mind.

Does the question or problem appear as a set of words or as an object?

Does the object or the set of words change colour?

What is the significance of that object or colour?

Has anything else appeared within the cube along with the question or problem?

Any of the above changes to the baseline could herald an intuitive answer starting to be formed.

Explore the changes or related object(s) carefully.

For example, when visualising a problem whilst practising this exercise, I was shown a tree with a door in its trunk. By opening the door and climbing up the stairs inside the tree, I was taken to a wall of pictures hanging there. I was particularly drawn to one picture that reminded me of a person who might be able to help me with the answer to my question. In so doing, I used my intuition to take me closer to the answer that I was seeking. If I were to draw a blank from that person, I could go back to that tree and explore further inside for other clues.

In following the exercise above, it is possible to tune into one's intuition, give it free range to flourish, and move a step closer to intuitive thoughts without needing the exercise. We all have an innate intuitive gift within us. In time you can tune into it and use it. Often the answers lie within oneself.

"As without, so within."

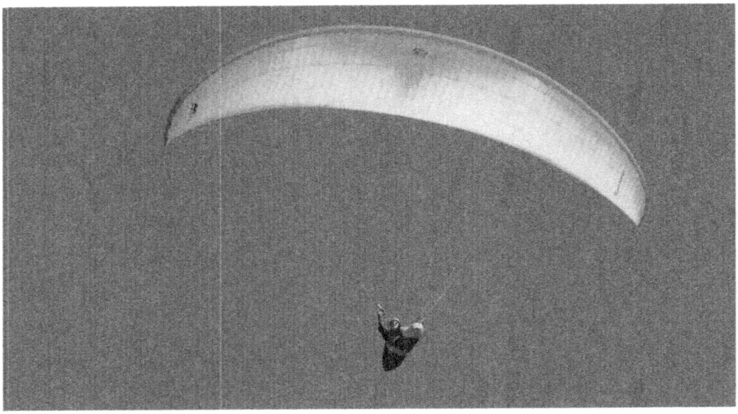

HOW TO CLEAR YOUR FEARS TO ACCESS YOUR INTUITION

By Amethyst Gray

"I must not fear. Fear is the mind-killer. Fear is the little-death that brings total obliteration. I will face my fear. I will permit it to pass over me and through me. And

when it has gone past I will turn the inner eye to see its path. Where the fear has gone there will be nothing. Only I will remain." — Frank Herbert, Dune

It happens to all of us. We all have worries; we all have fears. When those worries and fears become deep-rooted, we can become unable to get past them. They become all-consuming and even irrational.

It is believed that the vast majority – over 90% - of our fears and worries are nothing that we should be concerned over. However, there is always a small number that are real, of course.

There are many excellent techniques for dealing with fear. One of those is via the Emotional Freedom Technique (EFT), where you tap on critical points of the body, face and hands whilst holding a thought that bothers you or reciting a positive mantra.

But another technique to be used with caution is to 'face your fear'. However, this doesn't have to be literal or as dramatic as for 'Paul Atreides' from the book quoted above.

You can 'face your fear' by using your imagination or 'fear flipping' to help neutralise your fears.

Sit underneath your pyramid if you have one. Otherwise, find a quiet place and connect with the Great Pyramid of Giza or another place of power using the techniques above or in our previous books.

Once in your chosen space, you can relax by deep

breathing or using any other set of exercises that may help you to get into a deeply relaxing place. Now turn this into a 'safe space' by repeating the following mantra three times. "I am loved, and I am protected".

You are now ready to 'face your fears'.

Think of one fear or worry that is bothering you. Now expand it to the maximum extreme imaginable.

How does that feel? Is it terrifying? Now, remember that it is all in your imagination. It is not real.

How much better does that feel? It isn't real. It may never be real.

If you are still not sure, try flipping your fear. Take the opposite view of it. The best possible outcome.

How likely is that?

How much more likely than the fearful outcome?

Crystalise that positive possibility in your mind. Your fear has now gone over and through you.

Turn your thoughts to dissolving that fear completely. It doesn't exist.

It is a thought-form that will never take its form. Release the energy, absorb it and become stronger.

Reinforce the positive outcome, visualise it, make it the outcome you want to occur. The fear has gone. You are through the other side.

If the worries reappear, repeat the exercise until the

outcome is fixed in your mind's eye. Repeat for other fears and worries one by one.

Only you remain.

Now you have dealt with your fears; you are free to train and use your intuition.

ENHANCING YOUR INTUITION WITH PYRAMIDS AND CRYSTALS

By Amethyst Gray

If you don't have a physical pyramid to hand, don't despair. You can use the power of your mind to create one via visualisation.

Carefully smudge your space with sage (or similar) or use a crystal or metal sounding bowl, tingsha or drum to get rid of any spiritual debris that may be present in the space to purify it.

For even better results set up a crystal grid made up of double terminated (i.e. double pointed) quartz crystals or otherwise selenite sticks/wands along the edges of your pyramid (or other space) and at each corner an amethyst tumble stone or crystal. The quartz crystals or selenite need to be in line with each other along each side, terminated at each of the pyramid corners with the amethyst. If you are visualising the pyramid you can still grid out the area where you are going to sit.

You can hold an amethyst crystal, lapis lazuli, moonstone, apophyllite or sodalite in your hand or place on your third eye/brow chakra if you can do so safely and comfortably. These are the main stones of intuition.

Now get yourself comfortable and clear your mind. Listen to calming music if you need to.

For those without a physical pyramid:

Now visualise and trace out in your mind a square base large enough for you to comfortably sit in.

From each corner trace a diagonal triangular line one by one up to the apex of the pyramid.

When the pyramid is completely drawn in your mind and surrounds you in etheric space make a conscious connection to the Giza plateau and to the Great Pyramid there (or to any other pyramid there or elsewhere that you are drawn to).

For everyone:

Close your eyes if you have not already. Relax in your posture, place your hands in a comfortable position on your lap. Regulate your breathing, taking deep breaths into your lungs and chest cavity. Box breathing through your nose (if you can) or mouth otherwise may help you achieve this if you are able. This is achieved by breathing in deeply for four seconds, holding your breath for four seconds, breathing out for four seconds then holding for four seconds before repeating the process for two minutes or so (if you can safely do so). That's 4+4+4+4.

Once your breathing is deep but regular start to concentrate on your pineal gland, the tiny 'pineapple' in the centre of your brain. Visualise it being bathed in bright light. Imagine any hard deposits on its surface dissolving to reveal a healthy pinkie-red pineapple gland shimmering in the bright light.

Now imagine your pineal gland starting to radiate light back out and through to your third eye/brow chakra. Your inner Sun has been awakened and is ready to assist with your intuition.

Say the following mantra: "Please give me a message for my highest good and learning".

Empty your mind. Tune into your intuition.

What do you see?

What do you feel?

Are you receiving a message?

If so, then this should hopefully mean that your intuition is working for you.

Note that your intuition should not do anything to harm you, so if the message is potentially harmful to you or others go very carefully.

Repeat the messages step if required.

Once finished come gently out of your practice, open your eyes, drink plenty of water and if necessary, ground yourself by holding black obsidian, tourmaline or shungite in your hand(s) for a few minutes.

ACKNOWLEDGE-MENTS

The inspiration for the dissipation of fear was taken from *Dune* (1965) by Frank Herbert
The Bene Gesserit test Paul Atreides' humanity. If he fails the test he dies. To succeed he must master his fears. And so it is that in mastering your fears you can unlock a key tool of your humanity - your intuition.

All illustrations unless otherwise credited are photographs or diagrams by Amethyst Gray (c) 2021.

Cover illustration by A. Hargreaves.

ABOUT THE AUTHOR

Amethyst Gray

Amethyst Gray was born on the Isle of Wight, England and grew up close to Carisbrooke Castle. The Island, Arthur C. Clarke's Mysterious World on TV, fossils on the beach and crystals gave her a keen interest in history, hidden history and how everything came about. She was always good at Mathematics, so ended up taking a Physics degree at the University of London. That led to a career in IT before rediscovering her interest in crystals, alternative history and energy healing after moving to Wiltshire in the early 2010s. Now as well as being accomplished in IT, Amethyst teaches Angelic Reiki, practices Access Bars, Future Life Progression and Past-Life Regression in the vicinity of Avebury stone circle. She has given lectures on Atlantis and is in the process of publishing her Diana Garry book series. 'The Huntress' was released in August 2019 focussing upon Renaissance France, 'The Priestess', based upon Atlantis was published in March 2020. 'The Heiress' is slated for later in the 2020s with insights into survivors of the Titanic disaster.

ABOUT THE AUTHOR

Steve Nicholls

Steve Nicholls is a Guitar Teacher and spiritual being who lives with his wife in the middle of Wiltshire. He has been experiencing strange phenomena all of his life. He has a strong connection to Anubis and the Sphinx. He is planning to write his spiritual memoirs for publication in the next couple of years.

THE LITTLE BOOKS OF PYRAMIDS

This book series will introduce the reader to the world of Pyramids. It will provide the reader with an insight into the true origins of pyramids and their whereabouts on Earth, plus how to build a meditation pyramid then how to use pyramids for meditation, intuition and healing purposes.

The Little Book Of Pyramids

This book is an introduction to the world of Pyramids. It will provide the reader with an insight into the true origins of pyramids and their whereabouts on Earth. It will discuss the mysteries of the Great Sphinx and introduce spiritual concepts. The final section will allow the reader to build their own meditation pyramid from readily available materials to sit or crouch under in the Giza or Nubian configuration.

The Little Book Of Pyramid Meditation

The Little Book of Pyramid Meditation sets out to

introduce the reader to the practice of meditation with pyramids. It discusses the concepts behind meditation with relaxing illustrations. It then goes on to discuss one of the author's unique perspective on the spiritual aspects of meditation. It concludes with meditations utilising an etheric (imagined), or a constructed pyramid. The meditations are then enhanced using crystals,crystal skulls and crystal grids. It ends up with clear meditations making use of pyramids real or etheric and how to enhance them with crystals, crystal skulls and crystal grids.

The Little Book Of Pyramid Intuition

This book introduces the reader to the practice of intuition with (and without) pyramids. It explains the concept of intuition, its history and insights into intuition by the authors. It contains exercises to hone your intuition, purify it and to banish your fears to allow intuition to flow.

Printed in Great Britain
by Amazon

61992549R00031